Sports Illustrated KIDS

BIG-TIME RECORDS

BIG-TIME BASKETBALL RECORDS

Published by Capstone Press, an imprint of Capstone.
1710 Roe Crest Drive
North Mankato, Minnesota 56003
capstonepub.com

Copyright © 2022 by Capstone. All rights reserved. No part of this publication may be reproduced in whole or in part, or stored in a retrieval system, or transmitted in any form or by any means, electronic, mechanical, photocopying, recording, or otherwise, without written permission of the publisher.

SPORTS ILLUSTRATED KIDS is a trademark of ABG-SI LLC. Used with permission.

Library of Congress Cataloging-in-Publication Data
Names: Storden, Thom, author.
Title: Big-time basketball records / by Thom Storden.
Description: North Mankato, Minnesota : Capstone Press, 2022. | Series: Sports illustrated kids big-time records | Includes bibliographical references and index. | Audience: Ages 8–11 | Audience: Grades 4–6
Identifiers: LCCN 2021004245 (print) | LCCN 2021004246 (ebook) | ISBN 9781496695468 (hardcover) | ISBN 9781977159298 (paperback) | ISBN 9781977158932 (ebook PDF)
Subjects: LCSH: Basketball—Records—Juvenile literature.
Classification: LCC GV885.1 .S77 2021 (print) | LCC GV885.1 (ebook) | DDC 796.323—dc23
LC record available at https://lccn.loc.gov/2021004245
LC ebook record available at https://lccn.loc.gov/2021004246

Summary: Little excites basketball fans more than when a player hits nothing but net—except when that sweet shot sets a new record! Behind every big-time basketball record is a dramatic story of how a player or team achieved greatness. Air up your ball and get ready to learn about basketball's greatest players and teams and their record-setting triumphs on the court.

Editorial Credits
Editor, Aaron Sautter; Designer, Bobbie Nuytten; Media Researcher, Morgan Walters; Production Specialist, Tori Abraham

Image Credits
Associated Press: Al Messerschmidt, 25; Getty Images: Bettmann, 27, Focus On Sport, 11; Newscom: Adrees Latif/Reuters, 53, David Crane/ZUMA Press, 21, David Hahn/Icon Sportswire, 51, Javier Rojas/Pi/ZUMA Press, 39, Joel Lerner Xinhua News Agency, 13, Kyle Terada/Pool/ZUMA Press, 18, Mike Segar/REUTERS, 43, Mingo Nesmith/Icon Sportswire DIL, 42, USA Today Sports/Geoff Burke, Cover; Sports Illustrated: Andy Hayt, 49, Bob Rosato, 45, Heinz Kluetmeier, 31, John Biever, 20, 47, John G. Zimmerman, 16, John W. McDonough, 15, 35, 41, 48, 55, 57, 58, 59, Bottom of Form, Manny Millan, 5, 9, 23, 24, 33, 37, Neil Leifer, 29, Robert Beck, 10, Walter Iooss Jr., 7

All records and statistics in this book are current through the 2020–21 regular season.

TABLE OF CONTENTS

BEST OF THE BEST 4
BIG-TIME SHOOTERS 6
BIG-TIME ASSISTS 22
BIG-TIME REBOUNDERS 26
BIG-TIME DEFENDERS 32
DYNAMIC DUNKERS 38
RECORD-SETTING CHAMPS 44
BAD LUCK BALL 52
AMAZING BIG-TIME RECORDS 56

    NBA FINALS MATCHUPS AND VICTORS 60
    GLOSSARY 62
    READ MORE 63
    INTERNET SITES 63
    INDEX 64

WORDS IN **BOLD** APPEAR IN THE GLOSSARY.

Introduction

BEST OF THE BEST

Basketball is an ever-changing game. Ever since Dr. James Naismith invented basketball in Springfield, Massachusetts, for his physical education class in 1891, change has been a constant. In those first games, players were not allowed to dribble or run with the ball. **Substitutions** were limited. There were no **free throws** or 3-point shots. The ball had laces. The goals were actual peach baskets.

Eventually fans came to appreciate great dribblers like Bob Cousy, "Magic" Johnson, and John Stockton. They cheered for great 3-point shooters like Larry Bird and Klay Thompson. They marveled at dunkers like Rudy Gobert and Giannis Antetokounmpo. They admired the greatness of legends like Wilt Chamberlain, Bill Russell, Michael Jordan, and LeBron James.

As the game of basketball has changed, new standards are set. Though some records of the past seem unbreakable, fans thrill to each new groundbreaking effort.

During his time with the Chicago Bulls, Michael Jordan won six championships and was arguably the most popular athlete in the world.

Chapter One
BIG-TIME SHOOTERS

Putting the Ball in the Basket

To top the list of all-time greatest scorers in the National Basketball Association (NBA), a player needs extraordinary talent. He must be able to score against any defense. He must have a long career and few injuries that keep him off the court. Kareem Abdul-Jabbar had all these qualities and more.

Abdul-Jabbar was an instant success in the pros. This surprised no one. He was a success before he even joined the NBA. In college the 7-foot, 2-inch (218-centimeter) center dominated at the University of California-Los Angeles. He led the Bruins to three straight national championships.

The Milwaukee Bucks were the lucky team that landed Abdul-Jabbar in the 1969 NBA Draft. He quickly made a big difference on the team. In just his second year, Abdul-Jabbar helped the Bucks win the 1970–71 NBA title. He also captured the league's Most Valuable Player (MVP) award that season. In four of his six seasons in Milwaukee, he averaged at least 30 points per game.

Kareem Abdul-Jabbar started off his amazing NBA career with the Milwaukee Bucks in 1969.

In 1975 Abdul-Jabbar wanted out of Milwaukee and was traded to the Los Angeles Lakers. The Lakers' **franchise** was a successful one. They put great players around the big man for the next 14 seasons. With legendary Lakers guard Earvin "Magic" Johnson feeding Kareem the ball, L.A. lit up scoreboards and opponents. Abdul-Jabbar finally retired at age 42 with six MVPs, six NBA championships, and a record 38,387 career points.

> Kareem Abdul-Jabbar wasn't always known by that name. His original name was Lew Alcindor. He changed his name in 1971.

NBA Career Scoring

RANK	PLAYER	TEAM	YEARS	POINTS
1	Kareem Abdul-Jabbar	Bucks, Lakers	1969–1989	38,387
2	Karl Malone	Jazz, Lakers	1985–2004	36,928
3	LeBron James	Cavs, Heat, Lakers	2003–present	35,367*
4	Kobe Bryant	Lakers	1996–2016	33,643
5	Michael Jordan	Bulls, Wizards	1984–2003	32,292

*Stats listed are through the 2020–21 regular season.

Kareem Abdul-Jabbar's signature move was an unstoppable shot called the skyhook.

Diana Taurasi (#3) drove the ball down the court during a 2002 NCAA playoff game against Tennessee.

Like Kareem Abdul-Jabbar, the all-time leading scorer in the Women's National Basketball Association (WNBA) started as a college star. Diana Taurasi had a terrific career at the University of Connecticut from 2000–2004, winning three college titles with the Huskies. She was drafted by the Phoenix Mercury and led them to the WNBA title in 2009 and became the league's career scoring leader in 2017. She has also captured four Olympic gold medals with the U.S. Women's National Team.

WNBA Career Scoring

RANK	PLAYER	TEAM	YEARS	POINTS
1	Diana Taurasi	Mercury	2004–present	8,931*
2	Tina Thompson	Comets, Sparks, Storm	1997–2013	7,488
3	Tamika Catchings	Fever	2002–2016	7,380
4	Cappie Pondexter	4 teams	2006–2018	6,811
5	Candice Dupree	Sky, Mercury, Fever	2006–present	6,728*
6	Katie Smith	5 teams	1999–2013	6,452

*Stats listed are through the 2020 season.

College Marvels

Pete Maravich was a marvel with the Louisiana State University (LSU) Tigers. Playing for his father, Press Maravich, who coached the team, Pete could score from nearly anywhere on the court. And he always seemed to have a fancy move or trick shot up his sleeve. He averaged an amazing 44.2 points per game over three seasons with the Tigers. "Pistol Pete" went on to play 11 seasons in the NBA.

Kelsey Plum became the leading women's college career scorer in 2017. The University of Washington guard racked up 3,527 points with the Huskies. She then played in the WNBA with the San Antonio Stars and Las Vegas Aces.

Pete Maravich scored the most career points of any college player in history with 3,667.

College All-Time Leading Scorers (Women)

RANK	PLAYER	TEAM	YEARS	POINTS
1	Kelsey Plum	Washington	2013–2017	3,527
2	Kelsey Mitchell	Ohio State	2014–2018	3,402
3	Jackie Stiles	Missouri State	1997–2001	3,393

College All-Time Leading Scorers (Men)

RANK	PLAYER	TEAM	YEARS	POINTS
1	Pete Maravich	Louisiana State	1968–1970	3,667
2	Freeman Williams	Portland State	1975–1978	3,249
3	Chris Clemons	Campbell	2016–2019	3,225

Klay's Three for All

Klay Thompson comes from a talented family. His father, Mychal Thompson, was a star big man with the Portland Trail Blazers and Los Angeles Lakers in the 1980s. Klay also has two brothers who are pro athletes. One brother played for the Cleveland Cavaliers in 2011–2012. Thompson's other brother played outfield for several Major League Baseball teams.

Klay Thompson and Golden State Warriors teammate Stephen Curry are thought to be the best-shooting **backcourt** in the NBA. Together, they led the Warriors to championships in 2015, 2017, and 2018. In any given game, either player is a threat to go off from behind the three-point line. In 2016 Curry nailed 13 three-pointers to set the NBA record for threes in a single game. But during a 2018 game versus the Chicago Bulls, Thompson sank 14 three-pointers. Thompson is known for his quick release and picture-perfect shooting form. Smart fans wouldn't put it past Thompson or Curry to re-break the record again someday soon.

Most 3-Pointers in a Game, NBA

RANK	PLAYER	TEAM	YEAR	3-POINTERS MADE
1	Klay Thompson	Warriors	2018	14
2	Zach LaVine	Bulls	2019	13
2	Steph Curry	Warriors	2016	13
3	Steph Curry	Warriors	2016	12
3	Donyell Marshall	Raptors	2005	12
3	Kobe Bryant	Lakers	2003	12

On October 29, 2018, Klay Thompson set an NBA record by sinking 14 3-point shots against the Chicago Bulls.

Klay Thompson also owns the NBA record for points in a single quarter. In the third quarter in a game against the Sacramento Kings, Thompson poured in a record 37 points. He hit nine 3-pointers, went 4-for-4 in his other shots, and sank two free throws. For the game, Thompson finished with 52 points.

Free-Shooting Warrior

Shooting free throws is a skill anyone can practice in backyards, on playgrounds, and in gyms everywhere. But experienced shooters know that making free throws in practice and sinking them in games are two different things. In practice, there's no crowd noise or opposing players to distract them. But in a game, there may be an arena full of screaming fans. In practice, a shooter may be calm and rested. In a game situation, the shooter is likely tired, sweating, and nervous, with the game on the line.

Steph Curry, point guard for the Golden State Warriors, may be the best shooter the NBA has ever seen. He's well-known for his epic 3-point shooting. But he may be even better at the free throw line. Curry owns the record for best career free throw percentage. In fact, Curry is so good that opponents and fans are surprised when he misses a free throw shot. Curry's routine is simple at the line. One dribble. Slight knee bend. Picture perfect form and release. Swish.

Top Free Throw Percentage, Career

RANK	PLAYER	YEARS	TEAMS	FREE THROW PERCENTAGE
1	Steph Curry	2009–present	Warriors	.9069*
2	Steve Nash	1996–2014	Suns, Mavericks, Lakers	.9043
3	Mark Price	1986–1998	4 teams	.9039
4	Peja Stojakovic	1998–2011	5 teams	.8948
5	Chauncy Billups	1997–2014	7 teams	.8940

*Stats listed are through the 2020–21 regular season.

Steph Curry's (right) sweet shooting game brought him the league MVP trophy in the 2014–15 and 2015–16 seasons.

Steph Curry made 479 out of 547 free throws in his days at Davidson College. That was good for 87.6 percent.

Wonderful Wilt

When Wilt Chamberlain broke into the pros, no one had ever seen a player like him. Tall players were usually slow, clumsy, and not very athletic. But the 7-foot, 1-inch (216-cm) Chamberlain was thin and muscular. He could run like a deer and jump like a kangaroo.

Chamberlain began punishing NBA defenses right away. As a **rookie** for the Philadelphia Warriors, he scored 43 points in his very first game. For the season, he averaged 37.6 points per game. He also won Rookie of the Year and league MVP honors. Chamberlain dominated in scoring over the next three seasons. He averaged 38.4, 50.4, and 44.8 points per game during those years. He also set the record for points in a single game during that time, getting an even 100 on March 2, 1962, against the New York Knicks.

Due to his great height and jumping ability, Wilt Chamberlain's game was often played above the rim.

But one of the records set by "The Big Dipper" truly sets him apart from other players. Chamberlain broke the 50-point barrier an incredible 118 times in his NBA career. The next player on the list, Michael Jordan, did it only 31 times.

> Many all-time great players never scored 50 points in a single game. Such players include Earvin "Magic" Johnson, Bill Russell, Kevin Garnett, Julius Erving, Scottie Pippen, and Steve Nash.

Most 50-point Games, Career

RANK	PLAYER	YEARS	TEAM	NUMBER OF 50-POINT GAMES
1	Wilt Chamberlain	1959–1973	Warriors, 76ers, Lakers	118
2	Michael Jordan	1984–2003	Bulls, Wizards	31
3	Kobe Bryant	1996–2016	Lakers	25
4	James Harden	2009–present	Thunder, Rockets, Nets	23*
5	Elgin Baylor	1958–1972	Lakers	17

*Stats listed are through the 2020–21 regular season.

Postseason Point-Getter

LeBron James has played in a record number of playoff games. Through the 2019–20 season, he's appeared in 260 playoff games. James was always a major factor in the playoffs, upping his game when it was most important. As a result, his nearly 7,500 points in the NBA playoffs is a record.

James started his career playing for his hometown Cleveland Cavaliers in 2003. He led them to a surprise appearance in the 2007 NBA Finals. Though the Cavs lost to the San Antonio Spurs, it was a sign of things to come. In 2010 James moved on to the Miami Heat. He appeared in four straight Finals from 2011–2014, leading the team to two titles in 2012 and 2013.

LeBron James (left) led the underdog Cavaliers to capture Cleveland's first-ever title in the 2015 NBA Finals.

James then returned to Cleveland. There he led the Cavs to win the 2015–16 NBA title, Cleveland's first, against the Golden State Warriors. That season the Warriors had set the NBA record for best regular season record, going 73–9, but the Cavs beat them in the end. Though James has sunk a record number of playoff baskets, that championship run is considered James's greatest achievement.

LeBron in L.A.

LeBron James signed with the Los Angeles Lakers in 2018. In the 2019–20 season the Lakers had one of the best records in the NBA. Many believed that James was having one of his finest seasons ever. James's stats backed it up: 25.3 points per game, 7.8 **rebounds** per game, and a league-leading 10.2 **assists** per game. The Lakers beat the Miami Heat to win the NBA title. It was James's fourth championship.

Total Points in the Playoffs, Career

RANK	PLAYER	YEARS	TEAMS	PLAYOFF POINTS
1	LeBron James	2003–present	Cavs, Heat, Lakers	7,491*
2	Michael Jordan	1984–2003	Bulls, Wizards	5,987
3	Kareem Abdul-Jabbar	1969–1989	Bucks, Lakers	5,762
4	Kobe Bryant	1996–2016	Lakers	5,640
5	Shaquille O'Neal	1992–2011	6 teams	5,250

*Stats listed are through the 2019–20 season.

Points for Loyalty

Today's NBA players seem to be on the move a lot. Trades and **free agency** often make it seem like some players pack their bags for a new city just as they're settling in.

But that wasn't true of Karl Malone. He was a company man, and his company was the Utah Jazz. For 18 straight seasons, from 1985 to 2003, the stocky power forward filled the hoop for the purple and white. Malone could score down low, from midrange, and from the free throw line. His final season was played with the L.A. Lakers. But no player in NBA history ever scored more points for a single team than Karl Malone.

Kobe Bryant and Dirk Nowitzki were also loyal to their teams. Both poured in more than 30,000 points for their franchises. Bryant played 20 seasons for the L.A. Lakers, while Nowitzki logged 21 years with the Dallas Mavericks.

Karl Malone's career with the Utah Jazz included NBA Finals appearances in 1998 and 1999.

Kobe's Last Game

Going into the 2015–16 season, Kobe Bryant announced that it would be his last. Bryant was the Lakers' career scoring leader and had five championship rings. He didn't have much left to prove. Recent injuries had slowed him down and made preparing for each game painful. So at Kobe's last game on April 13, 2016, fans paid special attention. They were rewarded with one final magnificent performance. Bryant scored an amazing 60 points in a 101–96 win over the Utah Jazz. No player has ever scored more points in their final game.

Kobe Bryant's last game with the Lakers was on April 13, 2016.

Most Individual Career Points for a Single Franchise

RANK	PLAYER	TEAM	YEARS WITH TEAM	POINTS
1	Karl Malone	Jazz	1985–2003	36,374
2	Kobe Bryant	Lakers	1996–2016	33,643
3	Dirk Nowitzki	Mavericks	1998–2019	31,560
4	Michael Jordan	Bulls	1984–1998	29,277
5	Hakeem Olajuwon	Rockets	1984–2001	26,511

Chapter Two
BIG-TIME ASSISTS

The Magic Touch

At 6-feet, 9-inches (206 cm), Earvin "Magic" Johnson transformed the point guard position. Historically, the shortest players on the floor did the most dribbling and handling of the ball. Tall players stood closer to the basket so they could try to score. But Magic was a different kind of player.

Born in East Lansing, Michigan, young Earvin Johnson honed his game on the playground. He didn't have the prettiest shot, but he was a competitor, and he studied and practiced the game like no other. Following a title-winning college career at Michigan State, he joined the Lakers and made an impact right away. In his rookie season, his passing and clutch play helped the Lakers win the 1979–80 NBA title. Magic played with a lot of epic teammates including Kareem Abdul-Jabbar, James Worthy, Byron Scott, and A.C. Green. He made them all look good. During his 13 NBA seasons, Johnson dished out a record average of 11.19 assists per game.

> Magic Johnson won the NBA MVP award three times. He did it in 1986–87, 1988–89, and 1989–90. He also helped the Lakers to win five NBA championships.

Magic Johnson (#32) helped lead the Lakers to defeat the Philadelphia 76ers four games to two in the 1980 NBA Finals.

Career Average Assists Per Game

RANK	PLAYER	YEARS	TEAM	ASSISTS PER GAME
1	Magic Johnson	1979–1991, 1995–96	Lakers	11.19
2	John Stockton	1984–2003	Jazz	10.51
3	Oscar Robertson	1960–1974	Royals, Bucks	9.51
4	Chris Paul	2005–present	4 teams	9.43*
5	Isiah Thomas	1981–1994	Pistons	9.26

*Stats listed are through the 2020–21 regular season.

Everyday John

John Stockton wasn't a flashy player. In fact, he was almost boring at first glance. The Spokane, Washington, native had an ordinary haircut and attitude. But when you look closer, he was extraordinary. The 6-foot, 1-inch (185-cm) point guard wasn't especially fast, nimble, or athletic. But he was tough. He was feisty. He was determined. And he happened to be one of the greatest to ever play his position.

No one in pro basketball history has gained more career assists than Stockton. During his 19 seasons with the Utah Jazz, Stockton dished out more than 15,800 assists on the court. Stockton teamed with Karl Malone for 18 years to form a great one-two punch, and he assisted on most of Malone's buckets. The peak of Stockton's career came in the 1996–97 and 1997–98 seasons when the Jazz made it to the NBA Finals. But in both seasons the Jazz finished second to the Chicago Bulls.

John Stockton passed the ball against the Chicago Bulls in Game 1 of the 1997 NBA Finals.

Super Skiles

John Stockton recorded 20 or more assists in a game 38 times in his career. But he doesn't hold the record for assists in a single game. That record belongs to Scott Skiles, who had a game for the ages against the Denver Nuggets on December 30, 1990. In that game, the Orlando Magic point guard racked up an amazing 30 assists to break the previous record of 29 held by New Jersey Nets guard Kevin Porter. He also scored 22 points in that same game.

Scott Skiles hustled down the court against the Miami Heat in 1992.

Career Assists

RANK	PLAYER	YEARS	TEAMS	ASSISTS
1	John Stockton	1984–2003	Jazz	15,806
2	Jason Kidd	1994–2013	Mavericks, Suns, Nets, Knicks	12,091
3	Steve Nash	1996–2014	Suns, Mavericks, Lakers	10,335
4	Mark Jackson	1987–2004	7 teams	10,334
5	Magic Johnson	1979–1991, 1995–1996	Lakers	10,141

Chapter Three
BIG-TIME REBOUNDERS

Dynamic Duo

Bill Russell and Wilt Chamberlain had one of the most competitive rivalries pro basketball has ever seen. The two epic centers battled for ten seasons, from 1959 to 1969. The action was most fierce when Chamberlain was on offense and Russell was on defense. Chamberlain had a number of fake moves and shots he could pull off. Meanwhile, Russell seemed able to shadow a shadow and was a fearsome shot blocker.

Russell was born in Louisiana and attended the University of San Francisco in California. He was drafted by the St. Louis Hawks in 1956 and immediately traded to the Boston Celtics. Chamberlain grew up in Philadelphia and went to the University of Kansas before he was selected by his hometown Philadelphia Warriors in 1959. He moved to San Francisco with the franchise in 1962 and then was traded back to Philly to play with the 76ers in 1965. He spent his final seasons, from 1968–1973, in Los Angeles with the Lakers.

A major skill both of these players shared was rebounding. Chamberlain's height and jumping ability served him well when snaring missed shots. Russell was tall and athletic as well, but he relied more on footwork and technique to grab his rebounds. It's no surprise that the two players top the all-time list of NBA rebounding leaders.

Bill Russell (#6) battled Wilt Chamberlain (#13) during Game 3 of the 1969 NBA Finals.

When the two players met, it was common for Chamberlain to have a great game. But Russell's team often won in the end. Chamberlain and Russell faced off 143 times—94 times in the regular season and 49 times in the playoffs. Russell's team won 86 of those matchups. Chamberlain's teams won 57. In regular season games, Chamberlain averaged 29.9 points and 28.1 rebounds per game. Meanwhile, Russell averaged 14.2 points and 22.9 rebounds. In playoff matchups, Russell's numbers rose to 14.9 points and 24.7 rebounds per game. But Chamberlain's stats dipped to 25.7 points and 28.0 rebounds.

Russell is the all-time leading rebounder in NBA Finals games. He won 11 championships with the Celtics. Chamberlain is the second-leading rebounder in Finals history and won two championships. He won one with the 76ers in 1966–67 over Russell's Celtics. His second title came while with the Lakers in 1971–72, after Russell had retired.

Most Rebounds in Finals History

RANK	PLAYER	TEAMS	REBOUNDS IN FINALS GAMES
1	Bill Russell	Celtics	1,718
2	Wilt Chamberlain	Warriors, 76ers, Lakers	862
3	Elgin Baylor	Lakers	603
4	LeBron James	Cavs, Heat, Lakers	561*
5	Kareem Abdul-Jabbar	Bucks, Lakers	502

*Stats listed are through the 2019–20 season.

Bill Russell had 30 or more rebounds an amazing 13 times in Finals games. He notched 40 rebounds in two of those games, a feat that no one else has ever done. Wilt Chamberlain topped 30 rebounds five times in Finals games. Only one other player, Nate Thurmond, has notched 30 rebounds in a Finals contest.

Most Career Rebounds

RANK	PLAYER	YEARS	TEAMS	TOTAL REBOUNDS
1	Wilt Chamberlain	1959–1973	Warriors, 76ers, Lakers	23,924
2	Bill Russell	1956–1969	Celtics	21,620
3	Moses Malone	1974–1995	9 teams	17,834
4	Kareem Abdul-Jabbar	1969–1989	Bucks, Lakers	17,440
5	Artis Gilmore	1971–1988	4 teams	16,330

Cleaning the Glass

Moses Malone was a great defender at the rim. He was a relentless rebounder. Again and again he would jump, tip, and grab for the ball. The Houston Rockets center was especially effective while playing offense. His skills allowed Malone to set the record for most offensive rebounds in a single game. During a game against the Seattle SuperSonics on February 11, 1982, Malone grabbed a historic 21 offensive rebounds. He also snagged 11 defensive rebounds for a total of 32. He also scored 38 points in that game to lead the Rockets to victory. Malone's record-breaking performance was amazing, but not too surprising. After all, he led the NBA in rebounding for five straight seasons from 1980 to 1985.

Malone started his pro career in the ABA (American Basketball Association) in 1974 before jumping to the NBA in 1976. He had some great seasons in Houston before moving to the Philadelphia 76ers. In the 1982–83 season, he helped the 76ers win an NBA title alongside Julius "Dr. J." Erving and Maurice Cheeks.

Most Offensive Rebounds, Single Game*

RANK	PLAYER	TEAM	OPPONENT	DATE	OFFENSIVE REBOUNDS
1	Moses Malone	Rockets	SuperSonics	2/11/1982	21
2	Moses Malone	Rockets	Jazz	2/9/1979	19
3	Zaza Pachulia	Bucks	Nets	3/20/2015	18
3	Dennis Rodman	Pistons	Pacers	3/4/1992	18
3	Charles Oakley	Bulls	Bucks	3/15/1986	18

*Offensive rebounds were first counted as a separate category from total rebounds in the 1973–74 season.

While playing for the 76ers, Moses Malone (#2) grabbed the ball at the rim during Game 3 of the 1983 NBA Eastern Conference Finals.

Chapter Four
BIG-TIME DEFENDERS

Ministers of Defense

To be voted Defensive Player of the Year (DPOY) in the NBA, a player must be good at reacting. He must be smart. He must study his opponent. He must be tough. All of these qualities were found in two players that share the record for most DPOYs: Dikembe Mutombo and Ben Wallace.

Mutombo was a giant of a man. He stood 7-feet, 2-inches (218-cm) tall and weighed about 250 pounds (113 kilograms). His biggest defensive weapon was the blocked shot. Any player taking a shot near the rim had to be wary of Mutombo, who always seemed to lurk nearby. If a player didn't shoot quickly enough or put enough arc on his shot, Mutombo would slap it away. He led the NBA in blocks for three straight seasons, averaging about four blocks per game.

Wallace was a rugged defender. He had muscles that appeared to be chiseled out of stone. He wore a serious look and was as tough and hard to shake as could be. Wallace had his best seasons with the Detroit Pistons, where he won all of his DPOYs. In 2003–04, his defensive skill helped lead the Pistons to the title.

Dikembe Mutombo (right) blocked Kobe Bryant's shot during Game 4 of the 2001 NBA Finals.

Most Defensive Player of the Year Awards*

RANK	PLAYER	TEAM	SEASONS WON
1	Dikembe Mutombo	Nuggets, Hawks, 76ers	1994–95, 1996–97, 1997–98, 2000–01
1	Ben Wallace	Pistons	2001–02, 2002–03, 2004–05, 2005–06
3	Dwight Howard	Magic	2008–09, 2009–10, 2010–11
5	Multiple players have won twice		

*The Defensive Player of the Year award began in the 1982–83 season.

Man in the Middle

Tim Duncan wasn't flashy. He didn't show much emotion or talk trash to his opponents. He didn't wow fans with tricky moves, windmill **dunks**, or huge stats. He was, however, a very solid player. And he was a winner.

Duncan first came to the San Antonio Spurs in 1997 after playing college ball at Wake Forest in North Carolina. For the next 19 seasons Duncan manned the post for the black and silver. During that time the Spurs never had a losing season. While with the Spurs, Duncan made the All-Star team 15 times, and the Spurs won five titles.

The 6-foot, 11-inch (211-cm) forward-center was equally good on defense as he was on offense. He wasn't super quick. He wasn't overly athletic. What he did have was great footwork and technique. He always seemed to be in the right place at the right time. Duncan's many playoff appearances helped him set the record for most blocks in the NBA playoffs. He is the leader by nearly a hundred blocks, an impressive margin.

> Tim Duncan was born in the Virgin Islands. Before he took up basketball, he was a competitive swimmer.

Most Blocks, Playoffs (Since 1973–74)

RANK	PLAYER	TEAM	YEARS	BLOCKS
1	Tim Duncan	Spurs	1997–2016	568
2	Kareem Abdul-Jabbar	Bucks, Lakers	1969–1989	476
3	Hakeem Olajuwon	Rockets, Raptors	1984–2002	472
4	Shaquille O'Neal	6 Teams	1992–2011	459
5	David Robinson	Spurs	1989–2003	312

Tim Duncan's (#21) defensive skills helped lead the Spurs to victory in the 1999 NBA Western Conference Finals. He was later named the NBA Finals MVP.

The Answer

Allen Iverson was so quick and hard to guard that he gained the nickname "The Answer." Why? Because when the team wondered how to score points, they just gave it to Iverson, and they had the answer!

Iverson's quickness made him a force on defense as well as offense. He showed his ability during a May 13, 1999, playoff game versus the Orlando Magic. Iverson scored 33 points along with 5 assists and 5 rebounds to lead his Philadelphia 76ers to victory. But what really stood out was Iverson's 10 steals in the game. It was an NBA playoff record. Iverson stole weak passes, lazy dribbles, and was generally a thorn in the Magic's side.

Iverson finished his career as an 11-time All-Star and a four-time league scoring champ. He led the league three times in steals per game and won the 2000–01 league MVP award.

Steals in a Single Game, Playoffs

RANK	PLAYER	TEAM	OPPONENT	DATE	STEALS
1	Allen Iverson	76ers	Magic	5/13/1999	10
2	Mookie Blaylock	Hawks	Pacers	4/29/1996	8
2	Tim Hardaway	Warriors	SuperSonics	4/30/1992	8
2	Tim Hardaway	Warriors	Lakers	5/8/1991	8
2	Craig Hodges	Bucks	76ers	5/9/1986	8

Larry Kenon and Kendall Gill hold the record for steals in a non-playoff game. They are tied with 11 apiece. In 1985 Fat Lever of the Denver Nuggets once had an amazing eight steals in a single quarter.

Allen Iverson was drafted by the 76ers in 1996 and played the first ten seasons of his career in Philly.

Chapter Five
DYNAMIC DUNKERS

Rare Air

To dunk a basketball, a player has to jam it through a rim 10 feet (3 m) off the ground. Rudy Gobert can nearly do it standing flat-footed. The 7-foot, 1-inch (216-cm) tall center for the Utah Jazz has an amazing 9-foot, 9-inch (297-cm) standing reach. Gobert is also quite nimble for his height. His jumping ability regularly puts him high above the rim.

It's no surprise that Gobert holds the NBA record for most dunks in a season. In 2018–19 Gobert had 306 slams to break Dwight Howard's previous record of 269 dunks in a single season. That same season, another high flyer, Giannis Antetokounmpo of the Milwaukee Bucks, also passed Howard's mark. Antetokounmpo, who won the league MVP award that season, had 279 dunks.

Gobert and Antetokounmpo are both international stars. Gobert was born and raised in France while Antetokounmpo calls Athens, Greece, home. Each player regularly competes for their respective national teams as well as playing in the NBA.

Rudy Gobert (#27) dunked the ball during a game against the Los Angeles Clippers in 2019.

Most Dunks in a Single Season*

RANK	PLAYER	TEAM	SEASON	DUNKS
1	Rudy Gobert	Jazz	2018–19	306
2	Giannis Antetokounmpo	Bucks	2018–19	279
3	Dwight Howard	Magic	2007–08	269
4	Shaquille O'Neal	Heat	2004–05	255
5	Dwight Howard	Magic	2006–07	254

*Dunks were first counted in the 2000–01 season.

WNBA Jams

Lisa Leslie was one of the first big stars when the WNBA started play in 1997. Drafted by the Los Angeles Sparks, the 6-foot, 5-inch (196-cm) Leslie played college ball at the University of Southern California in Los Angeles. The Sparks had high hopes that Leslie would take the franchise to great heights. She did just that when she became the first WNBA player to throw down a dunk in a game.

The jam happened in Los Angeles on July 30, 2002, with the Sparks taking on the Miami Sol. After a Sol player missed a shot, the Sparks grabbed the rebound and passed the ball to Leslie, who was streaking across the midcourt line. Leslie raced down the lane and took flight off one foot. The ribbons in her ponytail flew as she rocked the rim with a right-handed throwdown. The crowd went wild. Leslie extended her arms, airplane style, and a wide smile broke out on her face as she ran back on defense. Her teammates hugged in celebration.

Since then, five other players have dunked in WNBA games. Candace Parker won the McDonald's High School All-American dunk contest in 2004. She was the only female player in a contest filled with guys. She dunked in college at the University of Tennessee, and she soon threw down big dunks in the WNBA.

Lisa Leslie went up for a big shot during the 2001 WNBA Western Conference Finals.

Brittney Griner may be the WNBA's most notable dunker. She dunked in her first game with the Phoenix Mercury in 2013. Griner, a 6-foot, 8-inch (203-cm) center, was born and raised in Texas. She dropped amazing dunks throughout high school and college. In the WNBA, she jams regularly and even threw down three dunks in the 2019 WNBA All-Star game.

WNBA Dunkers

RANK	PLAYER	TEAM	YEAR OF FIRST PRO DUNK
1	Lisa Leslie	Sparks	2002
2	Michelle Snow	Comets	2006
3	Candace Parker	Sparks	2008
4	Sylvia Fowles	Sky	2009
5	Brittney Griner	Mercury	2013
6	Jonquel Jones	Sun	2017

Brittney Griner was the number one pick in the 2013 WNBA Draft and shined for the Phoenix Mercury.

Slam-Jam Cambage

In 2012 Liz Cambage became the first woman to dunk in an Olympic competition. Playing for her Australian national team, Cambage dunked against Russia in the 2012 London Games. She has played professionally in Australia, China, and in the WNBA. In 2018 as a member of the Dallas Wings, she set the WNBA record for most points scored in a game with 53.

Liz Cambage (center) helped Australia beat Russia in the bronze medal game at the 2012 Olympic Games.

Chapter Six
RECORD-SETTING CHAMPS

Most Valuable Champion

Many consider Michael Jordan to be the greatest basketball player ever. However, although his **statistics** are impressive, he doesn't hold many major records. One reason for this is the fact that he retired twice. He sat out nearly five seasons of basketball in his 30s before finally retiring a third and final time.

But when Jordan was on the court, he was head and shoulders the best in the game. He played his best years with the Chicago Bulls in the 1990s. When he stuck out his tongue, everyone knew that Jordan was headed to the hoop and was going to score. It was just a matter of how.

When it came to playing for a championship, no player could guard Jordan . . . and no one seemed to want it more than him. Jordan's drive and desire to win are shown by a record he does hold: the total number of Finals MVPs. Six times in the 1990s, Jordan's Bulls won it all. Each time, Jordan was voted MVP of the Finals. No other player has come close to Jordan's six Finals MVP performances.

Basketball legend Michael Jordan made a high-flying shot during the 2003 NBA All Star Game.

Most NBA Finals MVPs

RANK	PLAYER	TEAM	NUMBER OF MVPs (YEARS)
1	Michael Jordan	Bulls	6 (1991, 1992, 1993, 1996, 1997, 1998)
2	LeBron James	Heat, Cavs, Lakers	4 (2012, 2013, 2016, 2020)
3	Magic Johnson	Lakers	3 (1980, 1982, 1987)
3	Shaquille O'Neal	Lakers	3 (2000, 2001, 2002)
3	Tim Duncan	Spurs	3 (1999, 2003, 2005)

Clutch Coach

Phil Jackson first tasted NBA glory as a player on the 1972–73 NBA champion New York Knicks. Though he was a role player, Jackson was smart. He was a hustler and a teammate who gave maximum effort.

After his playing career ended, Jackson took up coaching. Having learned a great deal from Knicks coach Red Holzman, Jackson began his coaching career in the Continental Basketball Association (CBA) and in Puerto Rico's pro league. He worked his way up the ranks until eventually becoming head coach of the Chicago Bulls in 1989.

Success soon followed for Jackson, who had superstar guard Michael Jordan on the squad. Jackson and his top assistant, Tex Winter, taught the "triangle offense." This strategy encouraged team play and took pressure off Jordan. The result was six championships in the 1990s for the Bulls. Jackson went on to coach the Los Angeles Lakers. There he won another five titles in the 2000s with great players like Shaquille O'Neal and Kobe Bryant. No NBA coach has won as many titles as Jackson.

Most NBA Titles, Coaching

RANK	COACH	TEAM	NUMBER OF TITLES (YEARS)
1	Phil Jackson	Bulls, Lakers	11
2	Red Auerbach	Celtics	9
3	Gregg Popovich	Spurs	5
3	Pat Riley	Lakers, Heat	5
3	John Kundla	Lakers	5

Michael Jordan (left) and coach Phil Jackson (right) held up trophies after the Chicago Bulls won the 1998 NBA Championship.

47

Irish Charm

No team had a run quite like the Boston Celtics did from 1957–1969. They won 11 championships in 13 seasons. They had Hall of Fame players including Bill Russell, Bob Cousy, John Havlicek, Sam Jones, and Tom Sanders. They also had legendary coach Red Auerbach. During their epic run, they were the best team in basketball. They were a **dynasty**.

A second wave of Celtics greats arrived in the 1980s. Players like Larry Bird, Kevin McHale, Robert Parish, and Dennis Johnson helped bring more championships to Boston. Most recently in the 2000s, the Celtics had the "Big 3" trio of Paul Pierce, Ray Allen, and Kevin Garnett. Together they brought even more glory to Boston. In all, the Celtics have won 17 NBA titles. The L.A. Lakers are the only other team to match that record.

The Boston Celtics celebrated winning the 2008 NBA Championship.

Rare Bird

Larry Bird was one of Boston's greatest players. In 13 seasons from 1979–1992, Bird held career averages of 24.3 points and 10.0 rebounds per game. He helped the Celtics win three championships. He also won three consecutive league MVP awards, in 1983–84, 1984–85, and 1985–86.

Larry Bird (#33) helped the Celtics win three NBA titles, including two over the Lakers.

The Celtics' biggest rival is the Los Angeles Lakers. The Celtics and Lakers have met in the NBA Finals twelve times. Boston won nine of those contests.

Most NBA Championships, Franchise*

RANK	FRANCHISE	NBA TITLES
1	Boston Celtics	17
1	Los Angeles Lakers	17
3	Chicago Bulls	6
3	Golden State Warriors	6
5	San Antonio Spurs	5

*Stats listed are through the 2019–20 season.

Husky Domination

For 865 straight days, the University of Connecticut women's basketball team never lost a game. But finally, on April 1, 2017, the Mississippi State Bulldogs downed the Huskies 66–64 in overtime to break the long streak.

The streak started on November 23, 2014, and lasted for 111 games—a college record. The streak was so long that it covered three separate seasons. A number of UConn hoopsters came and went in that time. The Huskies captured two college championships during their epic run.

There have been other long winning streaks in basketball. But the one the Huskies pulled off was one for the ages.

Longest Basketball Win Streaks

LEAGUE	TEAM	YEARS	GAMES
Women NCAA	University of Connecticut	2014–2017	111 games
Men NCAA	UCLA	1970–1974	88 games
WNBA	Los Angeles Sparks	2001	18 games
NBA	Los Angeles Lakers	1971–1972	33 games

The 2016 UConn Huskies went 38–0 and won the national championship.

The UConn women's basketball program has won 11 national championships, including four in a row from 2013–2016.

Chapter Seven
BAD LUCK BALL

Woeful Wolves

A team's wins and losses usually even out over time. But some teams just can't seem to catch a break. Take the Minnesota Timberwolves, for example. The Timberwolves started in the NBA as an expansion franchise in the 1989–90 season. Expansion franchises rarely have much success because it takes time to build a team.

Despite this, the Timberwolves did OK that first season, going 22–60. The next season, they improved to 29–53. There was hope in Minnesota. Sadly, the Wolves changed coaches the next year and dropped to just 15 wins. This began a long cycle of continued losing. The Timberwolves finally made it to the playoffs in 1997 thanks, in part, to a talented young player named Kevin Garnett.

With Garnett, the Timberwolves made the playoffs for eight straight seasons. But in 2007, Garnett moved to the Celtics. Garnett went on to win a championship with Boston. But the lowly Wolves returned to their losing ways. The team has only made a single playoff appearance since Garnett left.

> Minnesota hasn't always been a home to hoops heartbreak. The Los Angeles Lakers franchise actually started out in Minnesota. For 12 seasons, from 1948–1960, the Minneapolis Lakers were a great success, winning five league championships.

Minnesota Timberwolves players Chauncey Billups (left), Kevin Garnett (center), and Dean Garrett (right) took the bench after losing against the San Antonio Spurs in Game 2 of the 2001 Western Conference Playoffs.

Losing Streaks Abound

The team with the lowest winning percentage in a single NBA season was the 2011–12 Charlotte Bobcats. In a lockout-shortened year, the Bobcats went just 7–59 in 66 games. That's a win percentage of only .106.

Lowest Winning Percentage All-Time, Franchise*

RANK	FRANCHISE	WON-LOSS RECORD	WINNING PERCENTAGE
1	Minnesota Timberwolves	1,003–1,545	.393
2	Los Angeles Clippers	1,706–2,408	.414
3	Memphis Grizzlies	864–1,201	.418
4	Brooklyn Nets	1,533–2,089	.423
5	Charlotte Hornets	1,083–1,384	.438

*Stats listed are through the 2020–21 regular season.

Off Days

Every basketball game has a winner. Unfortunately, there is also a loser. That means that even the best of the professional players sometimes have off days.

Rasheed Wallace had more off days than most. He set the discouraging record for **technical fouls** in a single season (41) and a career (373). Off days are also what caused Andre Drummond to miss a record 23 free throws in a 2016 game. Even Hall of Fame point guard Jason Kidd had an off day when he had a record 14 **turnovers** in a single game in 2000. Tim Hardaway also had a bad day when he went for a record 0–17 from the field in a 1991 game.

Off days happen to everyone. But the best players know that tomorrow is a new day, and they make the most of it.

Most Turnovers, Career

RANK	PLAYER	TURNOVERS
1	LeBron James	4,592*
2	Karl Malone	4,524
3	Moses Malone	4,264
4	John Stockton	4,244
5	Kobe Bryant	4,010

*Stats listed are through the 2020–21 regular season.

Most Personal Fouls, Career

RANK	PLAYER	PERSONAL FOULS
1	Kareem Abdul-Jabbar	4,657
2	Karl Malone	4,578
3	Artis Gilmore	4,529
4	Robert Parish	4,443
5	Caldwell Jones	4,436

Rasheed Wallace (#30) tried to defend Kobe Bryant (#8) during the 2000 NBA Western Conference Finals.

Chapter Eight
AMAZING BIG-TIME RECORDS

Triple Double Kings

Russell Westbrook is a unique player. In his prime with the Oklahoma City Thunder, the 6-foot, 3-inch (191 cm) point guard could stuff the stat sheet like no other. When Westbrook was on fire, he often notched a **triple double**. That's a game where a player scores at least ten points, grabs at least ten rebounds, and passes for at least ten assists.

At the height of his stat-stuffing days, Westbrook once rattled off an amazing 11 straight triple doubles. He did this during the 2018–19 season. Westbrook had double-digit averages in points, rebounds, and assists for three straight years. That means he averaged a triple double over those entire seasons.

The only other player to average a triple double for an entire season is Oscar Robertson. He was a guard for the Cincinnati Royals and Milwaukee Bucks from 1960–1974. During his career, Robertson racked up the most triple doubles of all time with 181.

> Only four quadruple double performances have ever been recorded in NBA history. Nate Thurmond first did it for the Golden State Warriors in 1974 with 22 points, 14 rebounds, 13 assists, and 12 blocks. Alvin Robertson, Hakeem Olajuwon, and David Robinson are the other players to pull it off.

Russell Westbrook went up for a huge dunk against the Los Angeles Clippers in 2012.

Most Triple Doubles, Career

RANK	PLAYER	TRIPLE DOUBLES
1	Russell Westbrook	184*
2	Oscar Robertson	181
3	Magic Johnson	138
4	Jason Kidd	107
5	LeBron James	99*

*Stats listed are through the 2020–21 regular season.

More Incredible Records

Basketball is an amazing game. Here are some of the most amazing and hard-to-believe records you can find.

Youngest Player to Appear in an NBA Game

When Andrew Bynum made his first start for the Los Angeles Lakers on November 2, 2005, he was only 6 days past his 18th birthday. He only played until his mid-20s before knee injuries ended his career. But he was a force as a 7-foot (213-cm) center and won two championship rings. Other notable, slightly older 18-year-old stars to play in the NBA include Kobe Bryant, Tracy McGrady, Darryl Dawkins, and LeBron James.

Oldest Player to Appear in an NBA Game

Nat Hickey was the coach of the Providence Steamrollers in 1948 when he decided to put himself into a game. Hickey was just two days shy of his 46th birthday. He played only one more game before retiring. Kevin Willis suited up at age 44 for the Dallas Mavericks in 2007. Robert Parish played a season for the Chicago Bulls at age 43 in 1996–1997. Vince Carter also played until 43 with the Atlanta Hawks in 2019–20.

Andrew Bynum (#17) attempted a shot against the New Orleans Hornets during the 2011 NBA Playoffs.

Most Consecutive Games Played

A.C. Green was the NBA's Iron Man who played in an amazing 1,192 straight games. Green's streak started on November 19, 1986, when he played for the Lakers and ended on April 18, 2001, with the Miami Heat. During that time he also played for the Phoenix Suns and Dallas Mavericks.

Longest NBA Game

It took a record six overtimes for the Indianapolis Olympians to overtake the Rochester Royals, 75–73, on January 6, 1951. Ralph Beard and Alex Groza each sank 17 points for the winners. Arnie Risen scored 26 for the Royals in the loss.

Most Games Played in a Season, Individual

NBA teams play 82 games in a season, but somehow Walt Bellamy once played 88. In 1968–69 Bellamy started the season with the New York Knicks. Through the season's first 35 games he averaged a healthy 15.2 points and 11 rebounds per game, but then he was traded to the Detroit Pistons. The Pistons had played six less games than the Knicks at the time of the trade. So Bellamy played another 53 games that season. He averaged an even better 18.8 points and 13.5 rebounds per game with Detroit.

Best Record in a Season, Team

The Golden State Warriors were nearly unstoppable in 2015–16 as they set a single-season winning record at 73–9. That broke the 1995–96 Chicago Bulls previous record of 72–10. Unfortunately for the Steph Curry and Klay Thompson-led Warriors, they were stopped in the NBA Finals. LeBron James and the Cleveland Cavaliers upended the Warriors in an epic 7-game battle.

Most Free Throws in a Game Without a Miss

James Harden was nearly unstoppable in 2019–20. Many defenders instead tried to stop him by fouling him. On December 3, 2019, that strategy didn't work too well for the San Antonio Spurs. Harden shot 24 free throws—and made every single one—on his way to scoring 50 points. The Spurs, however, won in double overtime, 135–133.

James Harden focused on the basket to prepare for a free throw shot during a game in 2015.

NBA FINALS MATCHUPS AND VICTORS

1946-47	Philadelphia Warriors (4-1) over Chicago Stags
1947-48	Baltimore Bullets (4-2) over Philadelphia Warriors
1948-49	Minneapolis Lakers (4-2) over Washington Capitols
1949-50	Minneapolis Lakers (4-2) over Syracuse Nationals
1950-51	Rochester Royals (4-3) over New York Knicks
1951-52	Minneapolis Lakers (4-3) over New York Knicks
1952-53	Minneapolis Lakers (4-1) over New York Knicks
1953-54	Minneapolis Lakers (4-3) over Syracuse Nationals
1954-55	Syracuse Nationals (4-3) over Fort Wayne Pistons
1955-56	Philadelphia Warriors (4-1) over Fort Wayne Pistons
1956-57	Boston Celtics (4-3) over St. Louis Hawks
1957-58	St. Louis Hawks (4-2) over Boston Celtics
1958-59	Boston Celtics (4-0) over Minneapolis Lakers
1959-60	Boston Celtics (4-3) over St. Louis Hawks
1960-61	Boston Celtics (4-1) over St. Louis Hawks
1961-62	Boston Celtics (4-3) over Los Angeles Lakers
1962-63	Boston Celtics (4-2) over Los Angeles Lakers
1963-64	Boston Celtics (4-1) over San Francisco Warriors
1964-65	Boston Celtics (4-1) over Los Angeles Lakers
1965-66	Boston Celtics (4-3) over Los Angeles Lakers
1966-67	Philadelphia 76ers (4-2) over San Francisco Warriors
1967-68	Boston Celtics (4-2) over Los Angeles Lakers
1968-69	Boston Celtics (4-3) over Los Angeles Lakers
1969-70	New York Knicks (4-3) over Los Angeles Lakers
1970-71	Milwaukee Bucks (4-0) over Baltimore Bullets
1971-72	Los Angeles Lakers (4-1) over New York Knicks
1972-73	New York Knicks (4-1) over Los Angeles Lakers
1973-74	Boston Celtics (4-3) over Milwaukee Bucks
1974-75	Golden State Warriors (4-0) over Washington Bullets
1975-76	Boston Celtics (4-2) over Phoenix Suns
1976-77	Portland Trail Blazers (4-2) over Philadelphia 76ers
1977-78	Washington Bullets (4-3) over Seattle SuperSonics
1978-79	Seattle SuperSonics (4-1) over Washington Bullets
1979-80	Los Angeles Lakers (4-2) over Philadelphia 76ers
1980-81	Boston Celtics (4-2) over Houston Rockets
1981-82	Los Angeles Lakers (4-2) over Philadelphia 76ers

1982-83	Philadelphia 76ers (4-0) over Los Angeles Lakers
1983-84	Boston Celtics (4-3) over Los Angeles Lakers
1984-85	Los Angeles Lakers (4-2) over Boston Celtics
1985-86	Boston Celtics (4-2) over Houston Rockets
1986-87	Los Angeles Lakers (4-2) over Boston Celtics
1987-88	Los Angeles Lakers (4-3) over Detroit Pistons
1988-89	Detroit Pistons (4-0) over Los Angeles Lakers
1989-90	Detroit Pistons (4-1) over Portland Trail Blazers
1990-91	Chicago Bulls (4-1) over Los Angeles Lakers
1991-92	Chicago Bulls (4-2) over Portland Trail Blazers
1992-93	Chicago Bulls (4-2) over Phoenix Suns
1993-94	Houston Rockets (4-3) over New York Knicks
1994-95	Houston Rockets (4-0) over Orlando Magic
1995-96	Chicago Bulls (4-2) over Seattle SuperSonics
1996-97	Chicago Bulls (4-2) over Utah Jazz
1997-98	Chicago Bulls (4-2) over Utah Jazz
1998-99	San Antonio Spurs (4-1) over New York Knicks
1999-2000	Los Angeles Lakers (4-2) over Indiana Pacers
2000-01	Los Angeles Lakers (4-1) over Philadelphia 76ers
2001-02	Los Angeles Lakers (4-0) over New Jersey Nets
2002-03	San Antonio Spurs (4-2) over New Jersey Nets
2003-04	Detroit Pistons (4-1) over Los Angeles Lakers
2004-05	San Antonio Spurs (4-3) over Detroit Pistons
2005-06	Miami Heat (4-2) over Dallas Mavericks
2006-07	San Antonio Spurs (4-0) over Cleveland Cavaliers
2007-08	Boston Celtics (4-2) over Los Angeles Lakers
2008-09	Los Angeles Lakers (4-1) over Orlando Magic
2009-10	Los Angeles Lakers (4-3) over Boston Celtics
2010-11	Dallas Mavericks (4-2) over Miami Heat
2011-12	Miami Heat (4-1) over Oklahoma City Thunder
2012-13	Miami Heat (4-3) over San Antonio Spurs
2013-14	San Antonio Spurs (4-1) over Miami Heat
2014-15	Golden State Warriors (4-2) over Cleveland Cavaliers
2015-16	Cleveland Cavaliers (4-3) over Golden State Warriors
2016-17	Golden State Warriors (4-1) over Cleveland Cavaliers
2017-18	Golden State Warriors (4-0) over Cleveland Cavaliers
2018-19	Toronto Raptors (4-2) over Golden State Warriors
2019-20	Los Angeles Lakers (4-2) over Miami Heat

GLOSSARY

assist (uh-SIST)—a pass to a teammate that directly leads to a field goal

backcourt (BAK-cort)—a basketball team's starting guards

dunk (DUHNK)—when a player jumps above the basketball rim and throws the ball directly through the hoop

dynasty (DY-nuh-stee)—a team that wins multiple championships over a period of several years

franchise (FRAN-chize)—a team in its operating organization

free agency (FREE AYJ-uhn-see)—the ability of professional athletes to sign a contract with any team they wish

free throw (FREE THROH)—an unguarded shot taken from the free throw line by a player whose opponent committed a foul

rebound (REE-bound)—the act of taking possession of the ball after it bounces off the backboard or rim

rookie (RUH-kee)—a first-year player

statistics (stuh-TIS-tiks)—a collection of numerical data used to judge performance

substitution (suhb-stih-TOO-shuhn)—when a player on the court is replaced by another player from the bench

technical foul (TEK-nuh-kuhl FOUL)—a foul called for unsportsmanlike behavior

triple double (TRIH-puhl DUH-buhl)—when a player achieves double figures in three statistical categories (including points, rebounds, and assists)

turnover (TURN-oh-vuhr)—losing possession of the ball by a mistake or having it stolen

READ MORE

Frederick, Shane. *Basketball's Record Breakers*. North Mankato, MN: Capstone Press, 2017.

Jankowski, Matthew. *The Greatest Basketball Players of All Time*. New York: Gareth Stevens Publishing, 2020.

Storden, Thom. *Basketball's Greatest Buzzer Beaters and Other Crunch-time Heroics*. North Mankato, MN: Capstone Press, 2020.

INTERNET SITES

Basketball Reference
basketball-reference.com

National Basketball Association
nba.com

Sports Illustrated Kids
sikids.com

INDEX

3-pointers, 12
50-point games, 17

Abdul-Jabbar, Kareem, 6–8, 19, 22, 28, 29, 34, 54
Antetokounmpo, Giannis, 38, 39
assists, 23, 24–25

Bird, Larry, 49
blocks, 32, 34
Bryant, Kobe, 8, 12, 17, 19, 20, 21, 46, 54

Cambage, Liz, 43
Chamberlain, Wilt, 16–17, 26–28, 29
consecutive games played, 58
Curry, Steph, 12, 14, 15

Defensive Player of the Year (DPOY) awards, 32–33
Duncan, Tim, 34, 45
dunks, 38–39, 40–42, 43

free throw percentage, 14, 15
free throws per game, 59

games per season, 59
Garnett, Kevin, 17, 48, 52
Gobert, Rudy, 38, 39

James, LeBron, 8, 18–19, 28, 45, 54, 57
Johnson, Earvin "Magic," 8, 17, 22, 23, 25, 45, 57
Jordan, Michael, 8, 17, 19, 21, 44, 45, 46

Leslie, Lisa, 40, 42

longest game, 58
lowest win percentage, 53

Malone, Karl, 8, 20, 21, 24, 54
Malone, Moses, 29, 30, 54
Mutombo, Dikembe, 32, 33
MVP awards, 6, 8, 16, 22, 36, 38, 44, 45, 49

oldest player, 58

personal fouls, 54
points in career, 8, 10, 11
points in playoffs, 18, 19
points per franchise, 20, 21
points per game, 11, 43

rebounds, 28, 29, 30
Robertson, Oscar, 23, 56, 57
Russell, Bill, 17, 26–28, 29, 48

steals, 36
Stockton, John, 23, 24, 25, 54

Taurasi, Diana, 10
titles per franchise, 48, 49, 60–61
triple doubles, 56–57
turnovers, 54

University of Connecticut, 50

Wallace, Ben, 32, 33
Wallace, Rasheed, 54
Westbrook, Russell, 56, 57
wins by coach, 46
wins in a season, 59
win streaks, 50

youngest player, 58